In cooperation with William O. Petersen, Royal Joy Williams Chapter 1288 members Gwendolyn Tveter and Judy and Herb Johnson spent five years researching and compiling information for this book.

Our sincere thanks to those whose generous contribution of $1,000 or more made this publication possible:
John K. Notz, Jr.
Cedric and Tara Blazer
Conrad Petersen
Barbara Petersen
William O. Petersen
Gwendolyn Geyer Tveter
Cedar Point Park Friends, Williams Bay
Royal Joy William Questers, Chapter 1288
The Women's Civic League of Williams Bay

With special thanks to:
Joseph and Carol Schildgen Hays, who made their special contribution in honor of John Notz for his role as the first president of Black Point Historic Preserve, Inc. John's special resources and commitment as a profound scholar of Geneva Lake heritage have done much to add to the unique quality of life in this vibrant community.

This book is dedicated to the memory of Jane Browne Petersen, Herbert Brooks Johnson, and Richard Carr Tveter, all of whom worked tirelessly on the Black Point project but did not live to see the realization of the Black Point Historic Preserve, Inc.

THE BLACK POINT HISTORIC PRESERVE, INC.

On Monday September 26, 2005, after a ten year struggle, William O. Petersen,
the great-grandson of Conrad Seipp, legendary Chicago brewer and builder
of Black Point, stood on the front lawn of the estate looking out over the famed lake
and presented the property deed to State Tourism Secretary, Jim Holperin,
bringing to fruition the plan to convert the main house into an historic museum. Black
Point stands as an extraordinary time capsule detailing what life on
Geneva Lake was like during the late 19th and early 20th centuries – the era of
splendid summer estates and steam yachts. Black Point has been remarkably well
cared for and cherished by generations of the Seipp family and it is their hope that all
visitors enjoy and learn from its history and antiquities.

(Excerpt from the *Lake Geneva Regional News*)

CONTENTS

May this spot on beautiful Geneva Lake at all times appeal to the interests of the younger representatives, as it has for so many years to the older members of our clan… Let the spirit of our dear ones who are no longer in our midst be with us, and let us bear in mind that it is due to Grand-father Conrad Seipp and your revered and beloved Grandmother Catharina Seipp that we are privileged to be here and are able to enjoy today and let us hope for many years to come…this Good Old House and Place -BLACK POINT.

(an excerpt from *Black Point 50th Anniversary booklet* prepared in 1938 by Clara Bartholomay)

Opposite:
Conrad Seipp (1825-1890)

I. The Beginning

Born in Langen, Germany in 1825, Conrad Seipp was the youngest of Johannes and Anna Katharina Seipp's six children: Adam, Heinrich, Philip, Christian, Katharina and Conrad. By the time Johannes died in 1839 or so, Conrad had begun learning his father's trade of carpentry and was working the family farm with his brothers. But within less than a decade, turbulent political events began unravelling throughout Europe and Conrad's life would be changed forever.

The European Revolutions of 1848 first gained momentum in Sicily, then moved on to France, and soon came crashing down upon the rest of Europe. The upheavels were the direct result of the many changes that had been taking place in Europe during the first half of the 19th century. Politically, both bourgeois reformers and radical politicians were seeking reform in their nations' governments. Socially, technological advances were dramatically altering life for the working classes, just as a popular press was heightening political awareness, bestowing new ideas such as liberalism, nationalism and socialism upon the masses. What catapulted the events, however, were a series of economic declines and crop failures that left the vast majority of Europeans starving. Conrad's homeland was no exception.

At the time of the revolutions of 1848, Germany had been a collection of 38 states loosely bound together as the German Confederation. But the union was proving a dismal failure, pocked with regionalism and favoritism. For decades prior, calls for reform – for freedom and democracy – rang out, but were ignored.

By March of 1848, mass demonstrations were held in the southern and western regions of Germany, demanding freedom of the press, freedom of assembly and a national German parliament. Fearing the fate of Louis-Philippe of France, many rulers capitulated – others did not.

Maria Josepha Teutsch Seipp (1827-1866)

Conrad, who had been called into military service at the age of 20, was serving as a bodyguard for the Grand Duchess of Hessen when the rebellion began and he soon found himself at war against relatives and friends taking part in the uprising.

In the end, many historians believe the revolution became ineffective because of the overwhelming number of obstacles it faced and the mass support, as well as actual power, it lacked. Of reform the revolutionaries were able to accomplish, all were eventually abolished.

Perhaps it is for reasons such as this that Conrad no longer saw his future in Germany, but in the United States. In 1849, the young man packed his things, bid his family good-bye and headed to Rochester, New York. Here, he married a young woman from his homeland, Maria Josepha Teutsch, originally from Schifferstadt, Germany.

Soon after the nuptials, Seipp and his wife moved to Lyons (near Chicago, Illinois) where Conrad drove a beer wagon for Miller Brothers Brewery. But before long, Conrad set his sights anew. This time he and his young bride headed straight for the budding metropolis of Chicago, where for the next five years Conrad proved his acumen in business as a successful proprietor of a small hotel on the city's near west side. It was during this time, that Conrad's mother, older brother, Christian, and sister also left their homeland for the heartland.

Early in 1851, Conrad would stake a claim on 80 acres of farmland (nine miles from the southern edge of Chicago) where he, once more, moved his wife and their infant son, William (1851-1912) born that very year. Two more children were born on this farm, Elizabeth in 1852 and Frank in 1854, but died in infancy.

II. The Brewery Business

By 1854, Conrad Seipp had received his naturalization papers and pushed forward with his vision of the American Dream by purchasing a small pioneering brewery owned by Mathias Best. Located on Chicago's south side, the new owner moved his family to a small house opposite the brewery. There, the following year, his daughter Marie (1855-1937) was born. But happy tidings were soon overshadowed when, in 1855, a fire destroyed the entire brewery operations.

Unwavering, Seipp found a new location and rebuilt his brewery bigger and better than ever - this time constructed of brick and complete with underground cellars, a malt floor on the ground level and family living quarters on the second story. By the end of 1856, Conrad Seipp had six employees and his brewery had produced about 1,100 barrels of beer.

Two years later, his daughter, Hattie (1858-1948), was born. During that same year, Seipp entered into a partnership with M. Frederick Lehmann. With the additional capital that Lehmann brought to the business, the brewery, now called "Seipp & Lehmann", was greatly expanded. Within a decade or so, it was one of the largest and most innovative brewery operations in Chicago with 50 employees now making more than 50,000 barrels of beer annually.

In 1866, as Conrad's brewery continued to flourish, his wife of 18 years would pass away, leaving him a widower. Ever-determined to push ahead, Conrad would find a new matriarch within the year by marrying Catharina Orb, an emigrant from Westhofen, Rhein Hessen, Germany. Catharina would have five surviving children with Conrad, four of whom would not only perpetuate the family, but prove invaluable custodians of family history. They were: Emma [Schmidt] (1868-1942); Conrad J. (1883-1909); Clara [Bartholomay] (1871-1956); Elsa [Madelener] (1875-1962) and Alma [Hay] (1876-1966).

Opposite:
Portrait of Conrad Seipp

Catharina Orb Seipp (1847-1920)

As Conrad's family continued to grow, so did his business - helped, in great part, to the fact that the brewery was spared from the worst disaster in Chicago history, the Great Chicago Fire of 1871.

"There were lots of people ruined at that time," Conrad Seipp was quoted by the *Chicago Daily Tribune* as saying, "and I was lucky by having my brewery so far south that the fire didn't catch it. I always think when I see a poor fellow in the street. If he is to all appearances an honest man, maybe somebody has made money out of his misfortune. And if he chances to come to me I can't turn him away."

Seipp's partnership with Frederick Lehmann would suddenly end in 1872, when Lehmann was tragically killed in a horse and buggy accident. Despite this misfortune, the business continued to grow and by the late 1870s, was ranked as the fifth most successful brewery in the country, producing over 100,000 barrels of beer each year. In 1876, Seipp bought out his partner's shares, incorporated the business, and changed its name to the Conrad Seipp Brewing Company.

Right: The Conrad Seipp Brewery became one of the most successful breweries in the country due to strong ad campaigns, wide distribution, and underwriting inventions such as commercial refrigeration.

Below: A Conrad Seipp beer label commemorating the 1893 World's Fair in Chicago.

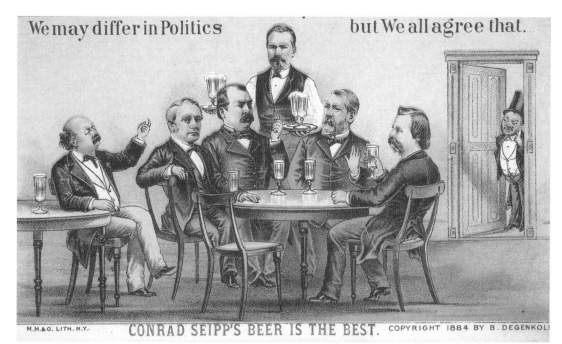

Within two decades, Conrad Seipp turned his small Chicago brewery, with a handful of employees, into one of the most successful breweries in the country, producing over 100,000 barrels of beer each year.

Seipp proved to be a shrewd and insightful businessman at every turn. His brewery, for example, was one of the few in Chicago which shipped beer outside city limits. This strategy not only tapped unexplored markets, but was greatly appreciated in the developing territories out West. Moreover, according to a *Chicago Daily Tribune* article from that period, Seipp's bottled beer had "...done more to reform the mining districts of the West than all the moral agencies that have ever been sent here. It has supplemented the use of stronger drinks."

Seipp also found great returns on the advertising dollar - during a time when it was thought there was little to gain from doing so. What's more, he had a flair for knowing his consumers. When horse racing tracks began to appear around the Chicago area, Seipp bought up parcels of land adjacent to the tracks and there he built company saloons. As his brewery business expanded as one of the most highly automated and mechanized industries in the country, Conrad Seipp made sure he was out front, leading the way. In 1881, he became even more powerful when he acquired West Side Brewing.

By the time Conrad Seipp passed away in 1890, he had taken a small brewery and built it into one of the most lucrative business ventures in the country. Following his death, the two breweries were sold to a group of English investors who merged Seipp's and several other malt houses to create the City of Chicago Consolidated Brewing and Malting Company, Ltd. In 1933, the Conrad Seipp Brewery made its very last bottle of beer, and shortly thereafter, the brewery was demolished to make room for a hospital.

In a *Tribune* interview following the beer tycoon's death, a colleague best summed up the self-made man as follows: "I knew him when he used to trundle beer in a wagon to customers and I have seen him at his palatial home on Michigan Avenue. From the first to the last he was the same, an openhearted, rugged, honest Teuton."

Designed by Adolph Cudell, the Seipp's main residence (c.1887) once stood at 3300 South Michigan Avenue in Chicago, Illinois.

III. The House in the City
Chicago, Illinois

Due to his great financial successes, Conrad Seipp was able to build two substantial homes in Chicago – the first in 1864 for his wife, Maria. It was a grand home built on South Park Avenue, one quarter of a mile west of the brewery.

The second was in 1887. With his family – and wealth – greatly increased, Conrad built an imposing residence at 3300 South Michigan Avenue with his second wife, Catharina. Along with many Chicago magnates, Seipp built his palatial stone manor just south of the business district on Michigan Avenue, known locally as "the sunny street that holds the sifted few".

At an estimated cost of $250,000, this magnificent residence, designed by architect Adolph Cudell, would be Seipp's most extravagant undertaking. Cudell, an Alsatian who immigrated to Chicago in 1873, had swiftly earned a reputation by designing a number of residences for some of Chicago's most prominent businessmen, including Cyrus McCormick and Perry Smith. In addition to the respect he gained as an architect, Cudell also offered something quite new for his millionaire clients. He and his partner, Alfred A. Lehmann, (the son of Seipp's former business partner) designed and manufactured furniture and interior millwork for residences – made possible by the booming Machine Age. In addition to his professional achievements, Cudell undoubtedly stirred Seipp's ardent and abiding interest in patronizing individuals from his native soil – a cause he and his wife, Catharina, would continue to champion throughout their lives.

Although the Michigan Avenue home would be in keeping with the industrialist's grand achievements, Seipp was known to have often remarked, "I wish I had my old home on South Park Avenue, where I could see the bright green lake, instead of a palace where I can see nothing."

So, it is little wonder that the very same year his lavish Chicago residence was being completed, Conrad Seipp commissioned Cudell to build a "modest" summer home for his family ninety feet above the shores of Geneva Lake on some land known to the Potawatomi as "Mekateneashe" and to the land's latest inhabitants... Black Point.

A Summer's Rest
at
KAYE'S PARK
Lake Geneva
WISCONSIN.

IV. The Lure of the Lake

The Seipp family was first drawn to the shores of Geneva Lake, as were many Chicagoans, to find solace and rejuvenation in the aftermath of the Great Chicago Fire. The small hamlet, with its plentiful lake and abundant natural resources, had enticed people from Illinois for decades. But with the vast devastation of the fire leaving hundreds of thousands homeless, and that very same year, the completion of the Chicago and Northwestern Railroad (now offering a mere two hour commute to a spring-fed lake and clean country air), Lake Geneva was fast becoming a thriving resort town.

In 1898, writer F.R. Chandler aptly described what the lakeside village was soon to become:

"Chicago capital and enterprise are here in abundance; the spirit of Chicago prevails here chastened by content and calmed by comfort, it is true but the flag of Chicago floats from every cottage, an invisible flag truly, but nevertheless a banner that signifies repose after activity and the enjoyment of the blessings of life."

One of the most popular resorts in the area (and the Midwest) was known as Kaye's Park, located six miles up the shore from the city of Lake Geneva. In an 1892 brochure, Kaye's Park boasted hotel and cottage accommodations for 200 people at a cost of ten to twenty dollars per week, two to four dollars per day. Along with the great outdoors, fresh vegetables from the park's gardens, fresh milk from the park's cows, and restorative spring waters, Arthur Kaye, proprietor of the resort, also offered his guests bathing, horseback riding, boating, fishing, driving, concerts, dancing, billiards, bowling, and "flirting."

A steamer, the *Arthur Kaye*, would transfer guests directly to and from the resort, meeting the morning and afternoon trains coming in from and heading back to Chicago, Milwaukee, and

Opposite Top:
The bustling docks at Kaye's Park Resort, Lake Geneva, Wisconsin, 1892.

Opposite Bottom:
Cover design of Kaye's Park brochure, 1892.

WINE LIST.

ARTHUR KAYE, Prop.

G. H. Mumm's extra dry	qts	$3 50
G. H. Mumm's extra dry	pts	1 75
Golden Cross	pts	1 25
St. Julien	qts	1 25
St. Julien	pts	65
Lolinsbergen	qts	1 25
Port Wine	qts	1 50
Port Wine	pts	75
Sherry	qts	1 50
Diana Wine	qts	1
Pure Grape Dry	qts	
Bass' Ale	pts	
Guinness Stout	pts	
P. H. Best Export Beer	qts	

☞ Waiters are Provided with Wine Cards and Pencils.

Meals Served in Room Extra.

HERALD STEAM PRINTING OFFICE,
LAKE GENEVA, W S.

Menu

SUNDAY, JULY 18, 1886.

FISH.
Baked White, wine sauce.

SOUP.
St. Julien.

BOILED.
Corned Beef and Cabbage.

ROAST.
Beef with Dish Gravy,
Mutton with Jelly,
Short Ribs of Beef, brown potatoes.

ENTREES.
Baked Macaroni, a la creme,
Fricassee of Lamb with Green Peas,
Peach Fritters, port wine sauce.

COLD.
Beef.
Potato Salad.
Mutton.

RELISHES.
Halford Souce,
Tomato Sauce,
English Mustard,
Chow-Chow,
Pickles.

VEGETABLES.
Mashed Potatoes,
String Beans,
Boiled Potatoes,
Turnips,
Beets.

PASTRY.
Blackberry Pie,
Jenny Lind Pudding, wine sauce,
Assorted Cake,
Lemon Pie,
Cream Puffs,
Vanilla Ice Cream.

Cheese.
Nuts.
Raisins.

Tea.
Coffee.
Milk.
Iced Tea.

Racine; "permitting the business man," as the brochure states, "to take his breakfast at the park, spend the day in the city, returning in the evening in time for supper."

The Seipps were among the many families who came to Arthur Kaye's resort in the wake of the fire and returned for some seasons following. However, in the autumn of 1887, twenty-eight acres on one of the highest points on the south shore of Geneva Lake became available near Kaye's Park. The land was part of Warwick Park, a 53-acre parcel developed by W. Anson Barnes, a professional landscape architect. Like other resort parks on the lake, Warwick Park offered cottages, tent camping sites and walking paths designed to attract vacationing Chicagoans.

But Conrad Seipp was more interested in the land and, as was his nature, wasted no time in acquiring it. Construction of the Seipp's summer "cottage" would begin that autumn.

Opposite: Resort's menu and wine selections, July 18, 1886.

Above: A scene from the shores of Kaye's Park.

Birds-eye illustration of the popular resort published in the Kaye's Park brochure of 1892.

V. The Summer Home
Lake Geneva, Wisconsin

Household furnishings tell a great deal about a family: values, tastes, attitudes, dreams and accomplishments. It is clear that the times spent at Black Point were not only enjoyable, but were revered.

(An excerpt from the *Black Point Feasibility Study*, prepared June 1995)

By the end of the nineteenth century, architects in the United States developed a rich, romantic, decorative style for houses known as Queen Anne, which combined classical features and design motifs with modern floor plans and liberating construction techniques. This popular style of architecture was used for many of the houses built during the 1880s and 1890s on Geneva Lake. Although the style often varies dramatically from one house to the next, one feature which is commonly shared in all Queen Anne architecture is the elaborate woodwork which came about as a result of the Machine – or Industrial – Age, when Americans became enraptured with the new technology which allowed factory-made, pre-cut architectural parts to be shipped across the country on a rapidly expanding train system. And few homes show this off better than what was known by the Seipp family as the "Big House" at Black Point.

Even though this summer home would cost substantially less (completed for about $20,000) than the Seipp's Chicago residence, the undertaking was immense. Not only did the enormous construction project require load after load of material being brought in by barge and horse-drawn wagons, Cudell's designs for Black Point called for intricate detailing both inside and out. Everything from the brewer's monogram etched on the beveled panes of the vestibule doors, to the tower room accessed by a passage door and steeply curved staircase, expounded the intricacy as well as the thoughtfulness of the home's layout.

Opposite:
The children's playhouse at Black Point was where imaginations blossomed for all of the children living on the estate.

Plans for the exterior of the magnificent Queen Anne house included steep-pitched gable roofs, decorative millwork and spindle work, balustrades, scroll cut cornice brackets, fretwork, fish scale siding, and expansive porches. Exquisite interior attributes included etched and stained glass; decorative glazed tile fireplaces (unique in each room on the first floor); stenciled and hand-painted wall and ceiling designs; as well as high ceilings and extensive windows and doors which allowed the residents of Black Point to enjoy the lake breezes throughout the house. In addition to a music room, a living room, a billiards room and a dining room located on the main floor, the second and third floors comprised twelve bedrooms (thirteen when including the room used for summer tutorials), all of which opened out into a center hall.

The enormity of the project was not lost on the mistress of the house. During a walk across the ice-covered lake as the winter construction began, Catharina Orb Seipp was said to have burst into tears when she saw the scaffolding and realized the sheer size of the project and what it would take to maintain such a home.

But the project pushed full-steam ahead and the following summer, while the house was being completed, the entire family settled into life at Black Point for the very first time. Fondly recalling the time in a booklet prepared for the 50th anniversary of Black Point, Seipp's daughter, Clara, wrote "During the summer of 1888 the whole family, including the Lefens family, lived in what is now the kitchen and laundry buildings, and although quarters were close, we were comfortable and had a happy time. Papa was in our midst and was tremendously interested in the construction of the house." (Sadly, Conrad Seipp would enjoy his summer haven for only one more season before succumbing to pneumonia in January of 1890.)

That summer, on the fourth of July, 1888, Emma Seipp hoisted the first flag at Black Point. This act would, from that point on, become a long-standing ritual signifying not only the family's arrival at the estate, but the beginning of summer, as well as the celebration of family milestones. Furthermore, the act became a much loved right-of-passage for the young men of Black Point. Upon turning fourteen years old, each boy was allowed to climb the tower of the Big House for the very first time in order to raise the American flag. It was an event greatly anticipated each summer.

Seipp's Sängerbund from the brewery met jointly with the Germania Männerchor of Lake Geneva to perform jointly.

Although the Big House was never intended to be lived in year round, the coal stove on the second floor helped the family remain at Black Point until mid-October.

Construction of the Big House was finally completed in July of 1888 and Cudell's designs for an open, flowing space of abundant light and gentle breezes, as well as ample room for quiet moments, countless guests and peaceful coexistence, became a reality.

The Big House was named Die Lorelei after the legend of a beautiful, golden-haired siren who, perched on a cliff overlooking the Rhine River in Germany, lured sailors to their death on the rocky shoals below. During World War I, however, for reasons of patriotic discretion, the family renamed the estate Black Point, taken from the ancient Potawatomi word, "mekateneashe" which alluded to the abundance of Black Oak trees first discovered growing on the land.

The main house at Black Point originally had gas lighting. A large tank outside held 20 to 30 barrels of machine gasoline and a pipe carried the highly volatile fuel to a converter in the basement. Through the use of pressure, liquid was changed to gas, which was then routed to lamps both inside and outside of the house. Electricity was installed in 1917, but a dual gas and electric system was maintained until 1924 – using gas during storms and other frequent power failures. The Big House was always intended as a summer home and had no central heating; and because of its construction, there was never any feasible way to adapt it for year round use. However, the furnace would take the chill out of the first floor; while a coal stove on the second floor helped to keep the house comfortable until mid October.

As customary for the times, the house was also designed with only one full bath on the second floor, which was most likely used by the older women in the family. Most personal hygiene was conducted in the bedroom and, of course, in the lake below.

Chamber pots were an essential part of each bedroom for the first several years at Black Point. In fact, a small room on the landing between the second and third floors was integrated into the design of the house specifically for these waste receptacles.

The summer home was furnished with the contents of the family's South Park Avenue residence, which they had recently vacated for their new Michigan Avenue house. By the time the furnishings were moved to Black Point, most items were considered out of fashion for the time, but instead of tossing them into a rubbish heap, the frugal minded millionaire sent the furniture north where they would serve the house for several generations. Today, Black Point is considered to have one of the most intact collections of Victorian furniture in the Midwest. The collection not only holds great importance due to its fascinating range of periods (almost entirely predating the summer home); but the types of furnishings found at the estate represent both typical and exceptional sights in a Victorian country residence.

A great many pieces at Black Point represent the Renaissance Revival style which epitomizes the Gilded Age of furniture design (1865-1885), popular following the Civil War. This was a period in American history when the economy was growing and the country was looking toward its future with confidence. This style (as reflected by the living room suite at Black Point) was often characterized by classic Greek, Roman, and Egyptian features, such as columns and cartouches, and tended to be large in scale. It also often mixed later styles, such as Gothic and Rococo into the designs. To the Victorians, "simple" was considered "uninteresting" and with manufacturers capable of turning out ornate detailing with speed and preciseness, the more elaborate the designs, the better.

By the latter part of the 1880s, however, the Arts and Crafts movement began to rebel against mass production and over-the-top ornamentation. Instead, the movement called upon artists, such as Adolph Cudell, to simplify their designs. Cudell did just that when he created the dining table with twenty matching chairs and the library table with four chairs now found at the summer estate. The Cudell pieces were originally used at the Seipp's Michigan Avenue house, but later were brought to Black Point along with other furnishings, (as well as a stained glass window) before the mansion was closed in the 1920s.

Several pieces at Black Point also embody what furniture styles would be typically found in a Victorian summer – or country – home, such as the simple, hand-painted, or "cottage" furniture found in the kitchen.

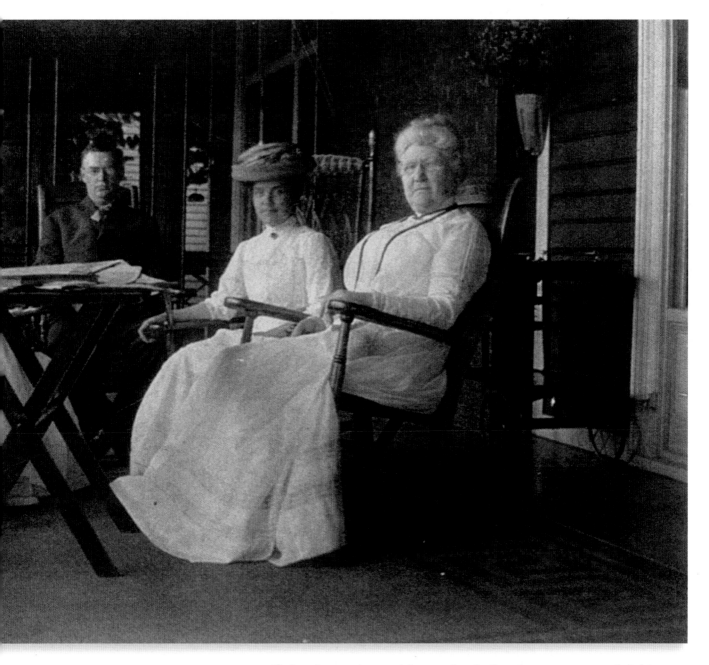

The home's expansive verandahs were where family and guests spent a great deal of time each summer relaxing, reading and socializing.

Garlands of grapevines and grape clusters were hand painted below the cornice and around doorways of this 18' by 28' room. In 1903, the Dining Room of the Big House was redecorated in honor of German relatives visiting America to attend the World's Fair in St. Louis.

Opposite: This sweeping staircase leads to the Tower.

–PHOTOS THIS SPREAD BY R. BRUCE THOMPSON

Nearly everything a visitor encounters at Black Point reflects not only a wide-ranging period in American history, but also a strong awareness of the family's history. An excellent example is the billiard table originally purchased for the Seipp's South Park residence. Bought as a means of entertaining refugees of the Chicago fire invited to stay at the family's home, the billiard table (which was later moved to Black Point in the 1880s) perfectly reflects the Seipp's desire to please their guests. Also in the Billiards Room, fireplace tiles portraying a child's Latin lesson and a large oil painting of a little boy impishly blowing bubbles at an old man smoking his pipe, imbue a strong sense of family and familiarity, openness and playfulness; just as the writing desks found in each and every bedroom at Black Point reveal the importance of exchanging ideas and reflecting on events.

From the moment the house first began to be used, Catharina Seipp treated it as a sanctuary for freedom and expression. Members of the third generation, for example, were allowed to add to the homey décor by plastering a wall of the Billiard Room with orange and blue Wheaties baseball players' photos from the 1930s.

The dining room porch (which could seat forty people) and the thirteen bedrooms – often furnished with twin beds and filled to capacity – also suggest that the house continually welcomed extended family members and friends to partake in the world of Black Point. In fact, the Big House often had thirty to forty people in residence, necessitating the scheduling of meals. As the family matriarch, Catharina (and later her daughter Emma) was frequently

responsible for coordinating at least sixty meals per day, seven days a week. Yet even with the demanding mealtime schedules, manners were never compromised. Meals in the country were as formal as those conducted in town – complete with linen napkins, silver, several courses, and a uniformed staff.

Part of the charm and enduring success of life at Black Point was undoubtedly due to the house, itself which always promoted socializing and accessibility, as well as diversion and contemplation – for times when adults and children were together and, of course, for the times they longed to be apart. Hand painted garlands of grapevines and grape clusters brought the out-of-doors in; while expansive verandahs – which allowed the family to play, eat, read, relax, and socialize – brought life into the open air. Important and ornate Victorian artwork always found a comfortable home next to generations of family photographs; books (a vital aspect of life at Black Point) and globes helped define an ever changing world, just as Old World customs and long-standing traditions helped define a family.

The Music Room was always alive with song when the family was in residence at Black Point.
–PHOTOS THIS SPREAD BY R. BRUCE THOMPSON

Above: The Living Room at Black Point has a lovely collection of East Lake furnishings and European artwork.

Below: The warm and inviting front entry of the Seipp's summer home.

To accommodate guests more readily, twin beds were used to furnish many of the bedrooms in the Big House.

—PHOTOS THIS PAGE BY R. BRUCE THOMPSON

Above: In the evening, the adults came and sat on the front porch of the Big House while Emma played piano in the music room.

Below: The Green Room was one of thirteen bedrooms, which clearly reveals the family's intent to welcome many guests to the estate.

VI. The Little House in the Big House

In the 1870s, Conrad Seipp decided that the average dollhouse was much too small for his family of girls. So, while living on South Park Avenue, he designed one with three sides entirely open and high enough so that all ages could enjoy it. Alma, the youngest, even had her own ladder so she could reach into the second floor bedrooms.

Traditionally, the dollhouse was only brought out during the Christmas season in Chicago. But after Catharina's death in 1920, the dollhouse moved to the home of whichever family member had daughters or grandchildren of the right age. And for six generations, the miniature house has been as important to the family's heritage as the Big House at Black Point. Over the years, just as with the summer estate, candlelight made way for electricity, rooms were re-arranged and gardens added. There have been weddings, dances and concerts and using vibrant imaginations, even more exciting events, such as attacks by Indians, fires, and burglaries. Even the boys of the family (who would not deign to play with actual dolls) took part in life around the dollhouse by taking on the role of Indian Chief or coachman, fireman or policeman, or whosoever was needed to play out an exciting event.

Throughout the years, because of constant use, much of the original furniture no longer exists and the dollhouse has undergone significant redecorations. However, the structure is currently undergoing major restoration to return it to its original 1870s style with the help of members of the Royal Joy Williams and Kishwauketoe Questers.

The Seipp Family dollhouse (c.1870s).

VII. The Family

Much has changed with the years. The times have changed and we of necessity with them. One thing, however, is the same today as in 1888... the loyalty of the family and the devotion all feel for one another. It is a spirit inherited from Grandmother... she who held us all together with a firm but loving hand. It was her understanding of problems confronting old and young, her keen sense of right and wrong, her love of the beautiful in living and doing for one another and her example to each and every one of us that has made our lives worth while and created the spirit of Black Point, such as we know it today.

(An excerpt from the 50th Anniversary booklet prepared in 1938 by Clara Bartholomay)

Each summer, the Big House was open by Memorial Day and closed by mid-October. The women, children, and Chicago staff came for the entire season while the men of the family normally commuted to the estate each weekend. From 1887 until 1919, transportation to Black Point was via the Chicago Northwestern Railroad – which chugged into Williams Bay, on the northwest side of the lake. From here, family and friends would head to their own private pier in Williams Bay to board the estate's steamer, also named *The Loreley*. With its flag flying, the steamer would transport its passengers to the estate pier located along its 2,700 feet of rugged shoreline. Here, luggage would be hoisted onto a wagon waiting at the dock and transported up the hill while family and guests made the final leg of the journey to Black Point on foot.

Each Friday, before the family began arriving at the depot, the steamer steered a course for Lake Geneva where household supplies would be purchased. On Monday mornings, the

*Catharina Orb Seipp and grandchildren. Top (left to right):
Catharina Bartholomay, Henry Bartholomay, Otto and
William Madlener twins, Alma Schmidt, Elsa Bartholomay,
Tessa Schmidt Reese, Al Madlener, and Ernst Schmidt.*

steamer would once again weigh anchor and transport commuters back to Williams Bay.

"In the early days," wrote Clara in the anniversary booklet, "we but rarely left the grounds, trips on the steamer 'Loreley' being the exception. How you would laugh could you see the excitement of a Friday afternoon in the gay nineties and the turn of the century! All of us in our prettiest gowns, large hats, parasols and silk gloves."

From the onset, Black Point was meant to be a retreat – a place where an individual's (especially a child's) personal development could be best cultivated and honed. Days were filled with sailing, swimming, riding, tennis, gardening, golf, playing games, a great deal of reading, and time with the tutors who taught a variety of subjects including German, Latin, botany, and other sciences.

Music also played a major role in the Seipp family. Emma Seipp Schmidt was an accomplished pianist, studying many years with world-renowned Chicago musicologist Bernhard Ziehn. Alma Seipp Hay was an equally

Above: The Seipp's steamer, The Loreley, met guests coming by train at its own private dock in Williams Bay.

Right: Emma (pictured) and her husband, Otto, together with Henry and Clara Seipp Bartholomay, were the estate's careful and loving guardians during the decades following Catharina's death in 1920.

accomplished violinist. Thus, nightly performances in the music room of Black Point took place throughout the season.

The Civil War march, "Skedaddles", sent the grandchildren to bed and birthdays were celebrated with a special march written by Elizabeth Sprague Coolidge, a Chicago acquaintance. Wagner was also very much a part of life at the estate and his music could often be heard wafting through the open windows of the Big House.

When the family celebrated the 50th anniversary of Black Point in 1938, a family orchestra was formed. With Emma at the piano and Alma on violin, a performance of Hayden's "Toy Symphony" was the highlight of the festivities. And although that tradition was suspended with Emma's death in 1942, the family found renewed interest during the 1980s and 90s as newer generations of musicians began to visit Black Point.

For the early generations of women at Black Point, another important pastime was mastering needlework. Hours upon hours would be spent crocheting bedspreads, knitting blankets, and embroidering linens - remarkably many of which (such as a tablecloth embroidered with the names of family and friends and pillow covers embroidered with the monogram "CS") continued to be used in the house until 2005.

Although pastime activities did vary with the newer generations, one that regularly disregarded the changing times was swimming in the lake. "Our costumes have changed from the sedate black silk

A family orchestra was formed for the celebration of Black Point's 50th anniversary.

Seated at the piano is Emma Schmidt.

Front row, from left to right: Meta Dunning, Marietta Chapin, Else Chapin, Alma Reese, Lowden Madlener.

Second Row: Bill Bartholomay, Sybil Reese, Nancy Madlener, and William O. Petersen.

Third Row: Conrad B. Petersen, Henry Bartholomay, Nate Osborne, Ernie Reese, and Claire Chapin.

Fourth Row: Edward Petersen on the horn, Alma Seipp as Manager, and Aunt Alma Hay on the violin.

and stockings to the comfortable athletic suits," wrote Clara, "but the fun at the lake and the laughter in the afternoon at the bathing pier are of the same volume. The shouts sound identical to those of the early years."

Fourth of July was another much loved event at Black Point. Picnic suppers on *The Nepenthe* (the family motor launch which eventually replaced *The Loreley*) were relished, just as putting on their own fireworks display always proved amusing, especially when memorable moments – such as the occasion when one family member was chased down the pier and into the lake by a blazing pinwheel – were created.

New memories were always being made at Black Point. There were countless weddings, anniversaries, christenings and birthdays which took place here during its 117 year history and every season meant new adventures to embark upon. There were canoe trips down the White River, hikes through the primeval forests. And each autumn, there was cider making and night visits to Yerkes Observatory. Life at Black Point was certainly never dull.

There were also daily chores for everyone, children included. Whether watering newly planted elm trees or picking raspberries, responsibility was a very important part of life overlooking Geneva Lake. This sense of responsibility becomes very clear when one looks to the individual members of the family and what many accomplished in their lives.

Alma Seipp Hay, for instance, used her own money to attend Wellesley. She was the first woman in the family to attend college despite some objections. After graduation, Alma left the comforts of home to go where teachers were desperately needed – Puerto Rico immediately following the Spanish American War. On the west wall of the Dining Room visitors to the estate will see a collection of corn kernel and seed collages which Alma brought back from her experiences there.

As stated previously, Catharina Seipp was very interested in calling attention to the issue of ethnic identity and the place it deserved in academic research. In 1904, for example, she established the Conrad Seipp Memorial German Prizes, awarded to three individuals who submitted the best scholarly work on the topic, "The German Element in the United States with Special Reference to Its Political, Moral, Social and Educational Influence."

Alma Schmidt Petersen, like her grandmother, Catharina, was heavily involved in community affairs, especially those benefiting the underprivileged. She was director of the Welfare Council of Metropolitan Chicago, as well as president of Hull House from 1945-1952. And just

Swimming in Geneva Lake was always a favorite pastime at Black Point. Pictured are Conrad W. and William O. Petersen.

Above: Emma Seipp Schmidt (1868-1942) and Dr. Otto L. Schmidt (1863-1935).

Lower: Ernst , Alma and Tessa Schmidt.

Opposite: Tessa Schmidt Reese (c. 1920s) standing at the estate's private harbor.

Alma Seipp Hay (1876-1966).

as her family before her, she supported many German-American causes and was awarded the Distinguished Service Cross from the Federal German Republic for her efforts on behalf of refugees following WWII. She was also honored with an honorary doctorate of Humane Letters from her alma mater, Mount Vernon College.

Alma's father and mother, Dr. Otto L. Schmidt and Emma Seipp Schmidt, joined by Henry and Clara Bartholomay, were responsible for Black Point for two decades following Catharina's death. Dr. Schmidt was outstanding in every field he entered. A highly regarded physician, specializing in the heart and stomach, he had the first x-ray equipment in Chicago and was associated with Northwestern University, Alexian Brothers and Michael Reese Hospitals. In addition, Dr. Schmidt also had a deep and abiding interest in history, serving as president of both the Illinois and the Mississippi Valley Historical Societies, as chairman of the Illinois Centennial Commission and the Illinois State Historical Society Library, as well as president of both the Chicago and German-American Historical Societies.

In addition to his love of history, Dr. Otto Schmidt also had a passion for sailing (undoubtedly spawned by his time at Black Point) and, in 1913, became president of the Inland Lakes Yachting Association (ILYA). During his presidency, he worked tirelessly to unite the ILYA with the Northwestern Regatta Association, which he also headed. He was president of the ILYA for twenty-two years until his death in 1935.

Dr. Schmidt's son-in-law, Dr. William F. Petersen, was another remarkable individual – also a medical pioneer, as well as a professor, author, and manufacturer. Dr. Petersen was one of the first in his field to study the effect of weather on people and diseases (meteor biology), was a professor of pathology at the University of Illinois College of Medicine and headed his father's company, Petersen Oven Company. In fact, his son, William O., remembers his father laying out plans for a new commercial oven in the boat house at Black Point. Endlessly active, retirement did little to slow the doctor down. Instead, he concentrated his energies on community health, chronic diseases, tuberculosis, alcoholism and conservation.

And when William F. Petersen wasn't advancing science, he was enhancing life at the summer estate. One year in particular, both young and old alike were both scared and bemused by a dragon which appeared in a pine grove near the western boundary of Black Point. The twelve foot long creature (made by the doctor out of plaster of Paris) had flashing eyes (powered by batteries), a noisy horn and was covered with scales. He would stand guard over Black Point for six seasons until wind and weather got the best of him.

Another great passion for Dr. Petersen, (like many family members before and after him), was horticulture. In fact, he was struck with an aneurism working on the grounds – fighting his arch nemesis – the invasion of the honeysuckle bushes always overrunning the property at Black Point. The problem was comparable to the garlic mustard and buckthorn invasions of today.

Above: For six years, a frightening creature haunted the woods at Black Point - a twelve foot long dragon, created by Dr. William F. Petersen out of plaster of Paris, batteries and an active imagination.

VIII. The Wind & The Water

Die Lorelei (The Loreley)
by Heinrich Heine

ORIGINAL

TRANSLATION by William O. Petersen & Gwendolyn Tveter

Ich weiß nicht, was soll es bedeuten,
Daß ich so traurig bin,
Ein Märchen aus uralten Zeiten,
Das kommt mir nicht aus dem Sinn.
Die Luft ist kühl und es dunkelt,
Und ruhig fließt der Rhein;
Der Gipfel des Berges funkelt,
Im Abendsonnenschein.

I cannot determine the cause of my melancholy,
There is a legend of old,
a story from ancient times,
That keeps running through my mind.
The air is cool and it is getting dark,
The Rhine is gently flowing;
The peak of the mountain is sparkling,
In the evening sunshine.

Die schönste Jungfrau sitzet
Dort oben wunderbar,
Ihr gold'nes Geschmeide blitzet,
Sie kämmt ihr goldenes Haar,
Sie kämmt es mit goldenem Kamme,
Und singt ein Lied dabei;
Das hat eine wundersame,
Gewalt'ge Melodei.

The loveliest young maiden is sitting,
Up there so wonderfully,
In the light her golden jewelry is glittering,
She combs her golden hair,
She combs it with a golden comb,
While singing a powerful song,
That has a wonderous melody.

Den Schiffer im kleinen Schiffe,
Ergreift es mit wildem Weh;
Er schaut nicht die Felsenriffe,
Er schaut nur hinauf in die Höh'.
Ich glaube, die Wellen verschlingen
Am Ende Schiffer und Kahn,
Und das hat mit ihrem Singen,
Die Loreley getan.

The boatman in his tiny boat,
Is seized with wild emotion;
He does not look at the rocky reef,
He looks only to the height above.
In the end, I believe, the waves
Swallowed both the boatman and his skiff.
And that is what the Loreley
Did with her singing.

Conrad Seipp's Loreley
–PHOTO BY THOMAS HAND KEEFE PHOTOGRAPHY

Although sailing was originally an activity to be mastered and enjoyed at Black Point, when Dr. Otto Schmidt arrived on Geneva Lake, the sport soon became a family passion.

In 1907, Dr. Schmidt first got his feet wet, so to speak, by ordering a Class A scow, which he named *Black Point*. The first Sunday after the new scow arrived, Otto Schmidt found some experienced friends and took to the water. His young son Ernst and his daughter Alma (who often sailed the estate's keelboat), were included.

In a moment familiar to all sailors of scows, *Black Point* was, by all accounts, going along fine, until the next moment, when those on board found themselves swimming alongside the scow which now lay upside down beside them. A passing launch lent a helping hand, taking Ernst and Alma back to the shores of Black Point where the youngsters made their waterlogged way up the front steps of the estate. It was here they encountered their startled grandmother.

Examining her soggy grandchildren with some dismay, Grandmother Seipp demanded an explanation. Upon receiving it, she gave standing orders that whenever her son-in-law set sail on *Black Point*, *The Loreley* was to "get up a full head of steam" and stand by for any eventualities. But Otto Schmidt was a fast learner and by the end of that same year, he went on to win the Sheridan Trophy Race (the first prize to be awarded for competitive sailing on Geneva Lake and one which is still presented annually) and was elected Commodore of the Lake Geneva Yacht Club the following year.

The position of Commodore, which he held from 1908-1909, was Schmidt's first undertaking with yachting organizations. In 1909, he accepted the job of Vice Commodore of the North-western Regatta Association and a year later became a member of the Executive Board of the Inland Lake Yachting Association (ILYA). This rapid rise was only the beginning. By 1913, Dr. Schmidt was Commodore of the Northwestern Regatta Association and also president of the Inland Lake Yachting Association. In six years, Otto Schmidt had progressed from an obscure name on the Lake Geneva Yachting Club's roster to a dominant figure

Led by Dr. Otto Schmidt (pictured left), an ardent sailor and competitor, many summer days at Black Point were spent in pursuit of a sailing trophy.

For other family members, an outing on the lake was simply a way to relax. Edward and Alma Schmidt Petersen aboard the Caligula (pictured right).

in one of the country's liveliest centers of sailing activity. From this powerful standing, he set about the task of uniting the two competing organizations he headed, which he accomplished eight years later.

In addition to his administrative successes, Schmidt was also victorious on the water, winning the esteemed Sheridan Prize a total of eight times – in 1907 and 1908, from 1913 through 1918, and in 1920.

And Otto Schmidt was not the only family member who had a passion for the wind and the water. His daughters, Alma and Tessa participated in regattas regularly. However, with most of the sailing fleets made up of men, the women were often timid in asserting their right of way. That is, until one day when Tilford Styvesant, a long time lake boatman, crewed with them and ordered Alma (who had the right of way) to stay her course. Doing so would mean hitting the oncoming boat, but stay she did. And, as the story goes, Alma was never denied the right of way thereafter.

Whether sailing competitively or boating recreationally, Geneva Lake had always been a source of great joy and infinite inspiration for the families of Black Point. In the 1930s, for example, the Petersen brothers were given a listless, old fishing boat which was said to cruise at a top speed of about eight miles per hour. This prompted the name *Walrus* and inspired their father (the dragon maker) to design a copper walrus to be placed on the transom of the boat. When out and about on the water, exhaust fumes were to exit good-naturedly from the creature's tail. However, before the first puff of smoke shot from the whimsical metal marine mammal, the plan was firmly censored by Mrs. Petersen and the boat exhaust was diverted to its mouth.

In 1937, when the Petersen family spent a summer enjoying a grand tour of Europe, Dr. Petersen became enamored with the fishing boats of Norway's Rana Fjord; miniature Viking boats (about 18 feet long), complete with red and white striped sails. Dr. Petersen couldn't resist. He bought one for $200 and had it shipped, at great expense, to Geneva Lake where he and his wife enjoyed sailing down the lake and then being towed home by one of the children.

Opposite: Dr. Schmidt (pictured here enjoying a few rare moments in repose during the LYA Regatta of 1925) was not only a passionate sailor, but a dominant leader in one in of the country's liveliest sailing regions.

Above: A Frisian Viking Boat was purchased in Norway by the Petersens while on a grand tour of Europe during the 1930s, and then shipped to the Lake Geneva Estate.

Opposite: *The estate's first steam vessel, The Loreley, would reflect only part of the family's desire to welcome friends and family to the inviting waters of Geneva Lake.*

Top: *Alma Schmidt and Jean Hippach who stayed their course.*

Lower: *The Nepenthe.*

The many brass name plaques in the Billiard Room of Black Point attest to the family's continuous love of boating – and in most cases their equal passion for the arts. The 45-foot launch which succeeded *The Loreley* in 1926 was named *Nepenthe* (a potion used to induce forgetfulness of pain and sorrow) from the Edgar Allen Poe poem, *The Raven*. Then there was *Ellida*, named after the ship of the protagonist, Fritjof, in a famous Norse saga. There was *Lively*, the estate's first motorboat; and the *Penguin*, a converted electric boat which got its name from its awkward posture when running. Over its long history, boats at Black point were named after Wagner operas, Frisian sea gods, ancestral sea captains, emperor's horses, explorers, and poets – all of which beautifully and lovingly complemented life at Black Point.

IX. The Black Point Estate

On September 15, 1994, Black Point was officially listed on both the National Register and the Wisconsin State Register of Historic Places. Jack Holzhueter, editor of the State Historical Society of Wisconsin's Magazine of History, declared the Big House on Black Point, "the best surviving example of the great summer houses in Wisconsin."

Everywhere you roam around Black Point's mature landscape of shady woodlands and well-worn pathways, terraced steps from the turn of the century and vivid gardens nurtured for generations, there is a permeating sense of a love of nature first cultivated by Catharina Seipp. "It was she who laid out the grounds, planted trees and shrubs, and developed the vegetable and flower gardens," Clara wrote in the anniversary booklet.

At the turn of the 20th century, Catharina would not only add land to the estate (acquiring properties which gave Black Point approximately 50 of the original 53-acres at Warwick Park), she and her son Conrad would also plant an extraordinary variety of deciduous trees, shrubberies and flower beds, as well as order deciduous and evergreen trees comprising 70 different varieties, to be planted on what would from then on be known as "Pine Hill".

Black Point's matriarch would also commission Olaf Benson, a landscape architect who was responsible for the designs of many of Chicago's parks, to help her with the enormous undertaking of turning the grounds of Black Point into a park-like setting where conservation went hand in hand with cultivation. Through the years, this commitment to Black Point's grounds would be continued by Catharina's descendants (as well as noted horticulturists)

Opposite:
The gazebo at Black Point overlooked the spring-fed waters of Geneva Lake ninety feet below.

whose love of the land and sense of stewardship has always been a cornerstone of life at Black Point.

In 1902, Catharina also purchased the neighboring 40-acre Baker Farm, largely for the purpose of supplying the Big House. She improved the farm by adding a cottage and several outbuildings which included: various storage sheds, a root cellar, poultry houses (for the farm's prize winning fowl shown during the summer fairs at Lake Geneva's Horticultural Hall and elsewhere); and barns that housed seven to eight milk cows, horses, sheep, and a variety of goats. A standard practice at Black Point was for all the children, at one time or another, to care for a goat.

In addition to land for grazing horses and goats and hay production, the farm also included an orchard with more than one hundred apple and cherry trees. Once harvested, these fruits, along with vegetables, eggs, and flowers, were shipped by train, supplying the family homes in Chicago throughout the year.

A large greenhouse, concrete hotbeds, and cutting gardens, along with extensive garden plots of perennial flowers, annuals, and vegetables were planted every growing season at Black Point. Of course, there were problem years – such as when 17 year locusts ravaged oak trees – but just as their patriarch was not easily thwarted by failure, the family found solutions to their agricultural woes at Black Point, such as bringing ducks in to gorge themselves on the garden pests until they could hardly waddle.

Cutting flowers (such as fragrant carnations, roses, snapdragons, gladiolas, and sweet peas) and vegetables (such as lettuce, beets, carrots, radishes, and tomatoes) were started from seed at Black Point, so care of the hothouses (along with cultivating the gardens, mowing the lawns and pruning the orchards) was an endless chore. The greenhouses were kept at a constant growing temperature by wood burning stoves, which meant the fuel supply had to be checked night and day. This often required stumbling out of bed at midnight, walking through the snow by lantern light – sometimes when the thermometer read 20 degrees below zero – and throwing wood into the stoves; only to repeat the process four hours later. In years to come, the chore was made a little less demanding by the addition of hand-fired coal burning furnaces.

Opposite: With the purchase of the adjacent 40-acre Baker Farm, the family was able to raise prize winning fowl which they showed at local competitions.

Above: Each child at Black Point was expected to raise a goat of his or her own.

A foreman and a farmer lived on the estate year round to tend to livestock and

to perform winter preparations for the coming seasons; and when extra help was needed, men from the town of Lake Geneva and the village of Walworth were hired to help. The going rate of pay was a dollar a day – a generous wage for the time. And if the workers had to come a long way by buggy or cutter they were paid $1.25.

Swimmers at the estate's Bath House.

There was always something going on at Black Point. When the lake was frozen over, a hustle and bustle of activity would commence as ice was cut for refrigeration in the Big House. Two hundred pound chunks of frozen lake were cut into 24" x 24" blocks and lifted with a jack onto a horse drawn sleigh which then hauled the blocks to the ice house, a sawdust-insulated building. The ice was then covered with marsh hay to prevent melting. Men filled the large, walk-in refrigerator at Black Point with nine blocks of ice weekly. If the lake was not frozen deeply, ice was cut from the Seipp's pond.

In addition to the Big House and the Baker Farm, in its prime, the Seipp Estate also included a large pier; a bath house; pavilions scattered across the property; a boat complex that included facilities for winter storage of the steamer; a steam pump and coaling facility; an icehouse; extensive greenhouses; a reservoir; and even a gravel pit at the east end of the farm property, which supplied material for the various roads and paths at Black Point.

Just like the children's heights recorded on a wall at Black Point, change at the estate occurred as part of a natural evolution. Gone is the building which housed a separate kitchen and servants' quarters. And two homes built by family members for year round use have been added. Gone are the expansive lawns, gardens, and savannahs which once spread to the shores of Geneva Lake. Chamber pots have been replaced by bathrooms, gas lighting by electricity.

Over the years, land was added, at one point totaling 90 acres… and then divided among family. The porches were widened to meet the needs of the expanding family and rooms were swapped when boats made way for horse-drawn carriages, and carriages made way for automobiles. Yet what remains at Black Point is an extraordinary testament to the power of family and tradition and to the enduring magnificence of life along the shores of Geneva Lake for seven generations.

Family members aboard the Lake Geneva Cruise Line boat, the Polaris at the 60th wedding anniversary of Edward and Zika Petersen.

Resource Guide

A Summer Rest at Kaye's Park, Lake Geneva, Wisconsin; Binner Engraving Company, Milwaukee, 1892. Walworth County Historical Society Collection.

Bartholomay, Clara. Black Point 50th Anniversary Booklet. 1938.

"Breweries." Encyclopedia of Chicago. 2006. Chicago Historical Society. 3 August, 2006 http://www.encyclopedia.chicagohistory.org/pages/164.html.

"Conrad Seipp Brewery." American Breweriana Association. 2006. 31 August, 2006 http://www.americanbreweriana.org/history/seipp.htm.

Darling, Sharon. "Chicago Furniture: Art, Craft, & Industry, 1833 -1983: 177, 183." Winterthur Portfolio, Vol. 22, No. 2/3 (Summer-Autumn, 1987): 195-197.

"Death of Conrad Seipp." Chicago Daily Tribune (1872-1963); 29 January, 1890; ProQuest Historical Newspapers Chicago Tribune (1849-1985): 6.

Frohna, Anne Celano. "Black Point: the Gift of Memories." The Week 24 May, 1998: 3A.

Lake Geneva Historical Society. Volume One, 1976: 133-136.

Lake Geneva Yacht Club, 1874-1974. 100th Year Anniversary Book. 1974.

Larkin, Larry. Full Speed Ahead: the Story of the Steamboat Era on Lake Geneva. June, 1972: 36, 39.

Lucas, Eileen. "Chapters from the Black Point Story." At The Lake Autumn, 1997: 32-36.

Lucas, Eileen. "Pieces from the Park." At The Lake Winter, 1998: 35-38.

"Obituary." Chicago Daily Tribune (1872-1963); 2 January, 1920; ProQuest Historical Newspapers Chicago Tribune (1849-1985): 19.

"Otto L. Schmidt, Physician and Historian, Dies." Chicago Daily Tribune (1872-1963); 21 August, 1935; ProQuest Historical Newspapers Chicago Tribune (1849-1985): 3.

Seipp, Edwin A. "History of Conrad Seipp and Family." Supplemented by Schmidt, Ernst C., 1944

Skilnik, Bob. The History of Beer and Brewing in Chicago, 1833-1978. Pogo Press, 1999.

Standish, David. "Green Mansions." Chicago Magazine July, 2001: p. 74.

Svendsen, Marlys A. Black Point Feasibility Study, prepared by Svendsen Tyler, Inc., June, 1995.

"W. F. Petersen, Physician and Writer, Dead." Chicago Daily Tribune (1872-1963); August 21, 1950; ProQuest Historical Newspapers Chicago Tribune (1849-1985): C6.

Wolfmeyer, Ann and Mary Burns Gage. Lake Geneva: Newport of the West 1870-1920. Lake Geneva Historical Society, 1976: 134 – 136.